Retail
INTERIORS

GLOUCESTER MASSACHUSETTS

ROCKPORT PUBLISHERS

For more beautiful work by these designers and others, see
these books, also from Rockport Publishers:
Commercial Lighting, by Randall Whitehead
Great Store Design, compiled in association with the Institute of
Store Planners
Great Store Design 2, compiled in association with the Institute
of Store Planners
Interior Color by Design, by Jonathan Poore
Interior Color by Design: Commercial, by Sandra Ragan

First published in the United States of America by:
Rockport Publishers, Inc.
33 Commercial Street
Gloucester, Massachusetts 01930-5089
Telephone: (978) 282-9590
Facsimile: (978) 283-2742

Distributed to the book trade and art trade in the United States by:
North Light Books, an imprint of
F & W Publications
1507 Dana Avenue
Cincinnati, Ohio 45207
Telephone: (800) 289-0963

Other Distribution by:
Rockport Publishers, Inc.
Gloucester, Massachusetts 01930-5089

ISBN 1-56496-509-0

10 9 8 7 6 5 4 3 2 1

Designer: SYP Design & Production
Cover image credit: Design by John Lum
                    Photography by Sharon Risedorph
                    (see page 12)

Printed in China

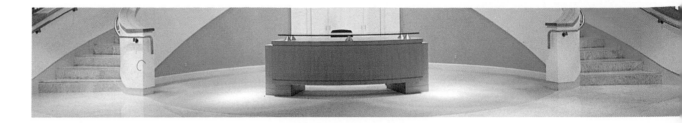

Introduction

Retail design might be called "the design of the times". Even the most traditional retail establishment must exemplify a contemporary zeitgeist, a design spirit that makes merchandise look new and desirable, appeals to the consumer's aesthetic needs, and ultimately persuades them to buy. This creates a paradox: strong retail identity versus versatility. How does the designer create a look that unquestionably signals the spirit of a clothier, chocolatier, or toy store while building in the essential ability to change displays for every new season or promotion? This book is filled with examples of retail design that effectively, approachably combines the timeless with the timely in a way that creates meaningful, market-savvy stores—from small boutiques to mega-retailers.

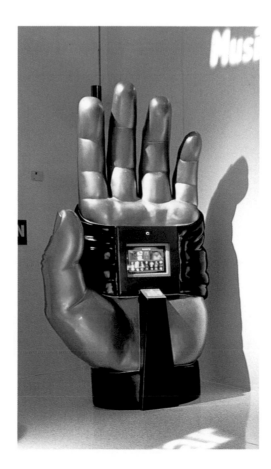

Design Fitzpatrick Design Group, Inc.,
New York City
Project Saks Fifth Avenue
SIXTH FLOOR MEN'S DEPARTMENT, NEW YORK CITY

Most dramatic about the renovation of design and
merchandising in Saks' men's department is the
newly opened windows on the Fifth Avenue side
overlooking Rockefeller Plaza. The formal Oval
Room and new windows anchor the plan.
Designer shops now occupy center stage in an
environment influenced by surrounding
architecture and art deco.

Design Fitzpatrick Design Group, Inc.,
New York City
Project Saks Fifth Avenue
SIXTH FLOOR MEN'S DEPARTMENT, NEW YORK CITY

Design Fitzpatrick Design Group, Inc.,
New York City
Project Saks Fifth Avenue
SIXTH FLOOR MEN'S DEPARTMENT, NEW YORK CITY

Design Jon Greenberg & Associates, Inc.
Project Marshall's
LIBERTY TREE MALL, DANVERS, MASSACHUSETTS

Striking a balance between Marshall's traditional off-price atmosphere and elements not usually found in a off-price environment, the remodeled Danvers Marshall's combines hard and soft materials, cold and warm color, and industrial-looking fixtures with flashes of "Marshall's Blue."

Design Jon Greenberg & Associates, Inc.
Project Marshall's
LIBERTY TREE MALL, DANVERS, MASSACHUSETTS

Design Jon Greenberg & Associates, Inc.
Project Marshall's
LIBERTY TREE MALL, DANVERS, MASSACHUSETTS

Design John Lum Architecture
Architect John Lum Architecture
Lighting John Lum Architecture
Project Urban Eyes Optometry Boutique #1

SAN FRANCISCO, CALIFORNIA

Because of the very small square footage of Urban Eyes' first store, the architect employed lighting as a way of making the space seem larger. Creating vignettes within the areas of light and dark visually expands the surroundings. A flexible, miniature track light system highlights the eyewear while producing a cross-hatched shadow effect. These dramatic contrasts produce an intimate atmosphere in keeping with the individualized attention each customer receives in this exclusive boutique.

PHOTO: SHARON RISEDORPH

A flexible track lighting system mounted above the ceiling line projects a vibrant halogen light to illuminate the structural column. The surface patina is textured with the impressions of the optometric instruments, antique eyewear, and the architect's and optometrist's handprints.

PHOTO: SHARON RISEDORPH

Design FRCH Design Worldwide
Project Liz Claiborne
SOMERSET COLLECTION, TROY, MICHIGAN

The new 8,400-foot Liz Claiborne prototype
segments the vendor's entire line with partial
walls. Ivory and cream colors, natural light oak
fixtures and flooring, sponge-painted walls, and
silk tussah walls meet Liz's signature colors in
aniline-dyed wood.

Design FRCH Design Worldwide
Project Liz Claiborne
SOMERSET COLLECTION, TROY, MICHIGAN

PETITES

Design Schafer Associates, Inc.
Project Carson Pirie Scott & Co.
THE SHOPS IN THE MART, MERCHANDISE MART, CHICAGO

Carson's new 50,000-square-foot anchor
(about half the size of a full-line Carson's) caters
to the predominantly professional, adult
population at this downtown location. The feel of
a specialty store conveys a sophisticated,
traditional, urban spirit.

Design Schafer Associates, Inc.
Project Carson Pirie Scott & Co.
THE SHOPS IN THE MART, MERCHANDISE MART, CHICAGO

Design Schafer Associates, Inc.
Project Carson Pirie Scott & Co.
THE SHOPS IN THE MART, MERCHANDISE MART, CHICAGO

Design Fitzpatrick Design Group, Inc.
Project Friars Square Shopping Center
AYLESBURY, ENGLAND

An oval aisle plan paralleled by merchandise walls puts all departments on the aisle with the correct fixture depth in this home furnishings store.

Design Fitzpatrick Design Group, Inc.
Project Friars Square Shopping Center
AYLESBURY, ENGLAND

Design Fitzpatrick Design Group, Inc.
Project Friars Square Shopping Center
AYLESBURY, ENGLAND

Design FRCH Design Worldwide
Project Rich's
NORTH POINT MALL, ATLANTA, GEORGIA

With roots in Atlanta since 1867, Rich's newest store makes use of pale colors, natural light, and artwork reflecting the southern state's current trends in residential decor.

Design FRCH Design Worldwide
Project Rich's
NORTH POINT MALL, ATLANTA, GEORGIA

Design FRCH Design Worldwide
Project Rich's
NORTH POINT MALL, ATLANTA, GEORGIA

Design FRCH Design Worldwide

Project Aca Joe
PERISUR MALL, MEXICO CITY

To change consumer perception from beachwear/T-shirt resource to an urban men's sportswear store anchored by jeans, the new design is influenced by English haberdashery. SDI redirected this look more toward young men and sportswear giving it Shaker-style fixtures and maple and Mexican tile flooring.

SLIM

ORIGINAL SLIM FITTING
FIVE POCKET JEAN.
NARROW LEG WITH
BUTTON FLY.

EL ORIGINAL CON
BOTONES Y CORTE
AJUSTADO.

EASY

EASIER FITTING
VERSION OF ORIGINAL
CLASSIC. ZIP FLY.

JEAN CLASICO
CON CIERRE.

LOOSE

AN UPDATED CLASSIC.
LOOSE FITTING WITH
WIDE TAPERED LEG.
BUTTON FLY.

EL MAS ACTUAL DE
LOS CLASICOS, CORTE
AMPLIO Y BOTONES.

BIG

WIDE LEG, ZIP FLY
AND BIG ALL OVER!

EL GRANDE DE
NUESTROS JEANS
CON CIERRE.

JEAN FINISHES

SUPER STONEWASH

FADED BLUE

DEEP INDIGO

MIDNIGHT

SLIM ACA JOE

LOOSE ACA JOE

EASY ACA JOE

BIG ACA JOE

Design The Pavlik Design Team
Project Marshall Field's
NORTHBROOK COURT, NORTHBROOK, ILLINOIS

Open design of this newly renovated three-level
Marshall Field's visually exposed the entire
expanse of each floor. Architecturally, the
275,000-square-foot store features huge
rotundas, promenades, and cruciform shopping
spaces. Proscenium arches create entrances to
the various apparel and home fashions
departments. Flooring consists of light marble
aisles inset with contrasting accents. Wall systems
and fixtures are movable for maximum flexibility.
Each department features varying color palettes.
Light residential woods are used in the fashion
accessories department, in contrast to the ebony
casework used in the fine home department. At
the heart of the store is a three-story atrium
incorporating escalators, elevator and a custom,
oversized Marshall Field's signature clock.

Design The Pavlik Design Team
Project Marshall Field's
NORTHBROOK COURT, NORTHBROOK, ILLINOIS

Design The Pavlik Design Team
Project Marshall Field's
NORTHBROOK COURT, NORTHBROOK, ILLINOIS

Design The Pavlik Design Team
Project Burdines
BRANDON TOWN CENTER, BRANDON, FLORIDA

Designed to enhance its "Florida store" image, this new 140,000-square-foot Burdines features an open floor plan with split escalators that allows customers a direct view through the entire store. Architecturally, the store recalls its native state through illuminated palm tree columns throughout the space and sand colored ceramic tile for main aisles. The pastel palette includes turquoise, seafoam green, shell whites and flamingo pink. Fixturing ranges from light wood tables to pink upholstered settees. Natural light is provided from the central oculus and cove lights.

PHOTO: MYRO ROSKY, FT. LAUDERDALE, FLORIDA

Design The Pavlik Design Team
Project Burdines
BRANDON TOWN CENTER, BRANDON, FLORIDA

Design Ohashi Design Studio
Architect Ohashi Design Studio
Lighting Alan and Joy Ohashi
Project Confetti Chocolat
SAN FRANCISCO, CALIFORNIA

Confetti Chocolat is a highly successful retail store combining gourmet coffee and candy sales in a festive environment with an Italian flavor. This was achieved by separating coffee sales, and carefully studying the layout of coffee equipment so that the queuing up for morning or lunch time coffee did not interfere with the more leisurely browsing for candy. The lighting was designed to be high key, focusing spots, floods, and wall washers on only the merchandise or serving counters to create highlights and shadows for a lively retail environment.

PHOTO: RUSSELL ABRAHAM

Design Nicholas P. Zalany/Richard R. Jencen Associates
Lighting Nicholas P. Zalany/Richard R. Jencen Associates
Project Karat Gold
NORTH ANDOVER, MASSACHUSETTS

Peripheral showcases are angled to maximize linear display footage while adding visual interest. Gold jewelry is accentuated with a black background and a combination of daylight, fluorescent, and halogen lighting. The fluorescent lights are hidden inside the floor showcases, while the halogens are suspended low enough to shine closer to the cases. Since showcases along the perimeter of the store did not allow enough room for large fluorescent strips, halogens were used both to brighten these cases and to accent the jewelry.

PHOTO: ALEX BEATTY

Design John Lum Architecture ▶
Project Urban Eyes Optometry Boutique #1
Architect John Lum Architecture
Lighting John Lum Architecture
SAN FRANCISCO, CALIFORNIA

A close-up view of shadow play and progressive eyewear treatment.

PHOTO: SHARON RISEDORPH

Design Paul Haigh and Barbara Haigh ▼
Project Mikasa...lifestyle
Architect Haigh Architects Designers
Lighting Paul Haigh
SECAUCUS, NEW JERSEY

The view of the interior shows the displays and check-out area. An ambient system of industrial fluorescent fixtures positioned to reflect from the underside of the roof deck is balanced by a grid of Par 38 spots on extension wands, aimed to highlight the displayed merchandise.

PHOTO: ELLIOT KAUFMAN

Design Jon Greenberg & Associates, Inc.
Project Scott Shuptrine
TROY, MICHIGAN

Once a brown brick furniture showroom, this home fashions store now features eclectic niche presentations, a gray and gold marble walkway and furniture style groups presented on special pods 26 feet in diameter.

Design Jon Greenberg & Associates, Inc.
Project Scott Shuptrine
TROY, MICHIGAN

Design Jon Greenberg & Associates, Inc.
Project Detroit Institute of Arts Museum Shop
SOMERSET COLLECTION, TROY, MICHIGAN

Recreating the authenticity of the Detroit Institute
of Arts' architectural heritage and rich cultural
imagery, the 1,800-square-foot museum shop
design is separated into "indoor" and "outdoor"
areas. Art pieces and historical references
abound.

Design Schafer Associates, Inc.

Project Gran Bazar

PLAZA TOLUCA, TOLUCA, MEXICO

A 240,000-square-foot, one-level space large enough to fit four football fields, Gran Bazar features over 50 cashwraps, 2,000 shopping carts, and employee runners on roller skates. To organize the huge space into an easy-to-shop, fun environment took a color-coded plan of three merchandise worlds, strong graphics, and a flexible fixturing system to handle product that sometimes turns over within a few hours.

Design Schafer Associates, Inc.
Project Gran Bazar
PLAZA TOLUCA, TOLUCA, MEXICO

Design Ronnette Riley Architect
Project New World Coffee
THIRD AVENUE, NEW YORK CITY

The design of New World Coffee evokes the warmth of experience and aroma associated with authentic espresso beverages. Earthy and coffee tones, stone, and wood come into play, as do a green-gold back-drop contrasted by cream-colored walls and floor. Lighting and a sharply angled counter punctuated by pendant lights along its edge draw the eye into the store from the streetfront.

COFFEE BEANS

Coffee Family	Varietal or Blend	Pound	1/2 Pound
Americas	Guatemala Antigua	$8.19	$4.09
	Colombia Supremo	$6.49	$3.25
		$7.79	$3.89
Africa & Arabia	Kenya AA	$9.49	$4.75
	Ethiopia Yergacheffe	$10.90	$5.49
Pacific	Sulawesi	$7.39	$3.69
	Java Estate		
Blends	Espresso Blend	$8.19	$4.09
	Espresso Blend Decaf	$9.29	$4.6
	New World Blend	$7.39	$
	New World Blend	$8.49	$4.25

Design Ronnette Riley Architect
Project New World Coffee
THIRD AVENUE, NEW YORK CITY

Design Lee Stout, Inc., New York City

Project Steuben at the Greenbrier
THE GREENBRIER RESORT, WHITE SULPHER SPRINGS,
WEST VIRGINIA

The Steuben Glass store at the historic resort
hotel is sophisticated yet relaxed enough to
welcome those clothed casually for golf and
leisure. Virtually every light in the space is
directed onto the glass, and most ambient
illumination is a result of reflections and refractions
from the light beams hitting the glass objects.

Design Ronnette Riley Architect
Project New World Coffee
HACKENSACK, NEW JERSEY

The design objective was to translate the interior of New World Coffee's shop to a freestanding pavilion. Earth colors of cherry wood, copper-toned bronze, and black steel from New World's shops are incorporated into the kiosk design. Angled bronze columns and glass display cabinets mark the corners of the structure, while flooring of Rosa Aura marble is inlaid with terra-cotta veining. Angular pendant light fixtures hang above the counter, highlighting the custom bronze work and accent panels. Open to the skylit atrium above, the kiosk is visible from all levels of the mall.

PHOTO: DUB ROGERS, NEW YORK CITY

Design The Pavlick Design Team
Project KidsFun
NORTHCOURT, TAMPA, FLORIDA

Designed for kids twelve years and under and their parents, this play center kicks off with an illuminated, three-story kite-shaped entry arch and follows through on the fun theme with games, rides, bold colors and patterns, zigzag walls, undulating forms, and skewed aisles. A glass-enclosed parents lounge is centrally located and offers maximum visibility along with peace and quiet.

Design Design Forum, Dayton, OH
Project Incredible Universe
TOWN CENTER LOOP WEST, WILSONVILLE, OREGON

Taking the category "killer approach" to a new level, Incredible Universe covers a total of 160,000 square feet of combined selling and warehouse space for consumer electronics. A host of shops are tied together with vibrant splashes of color, bright neon lights, and oversized signage and graphics perhaps best described as animated neon sculptures of the products within each department.

Design Design Forum, Dayton, OH
Project Incredible Universe
TOWN CENTER LOOP WEST, WILSONVILLE, OREGON

Design Design Forum, Dayton, OH
Project Incredible Universe
TOWN CENTER LOOP WEST, WILSONVILLE, OREGON

Design Kiku Obata & Company, Inc.
Project Big Future Interactive Theme House
CLAYTON ROAD, ST. LOUIS, MISSOURI

This 13,000-square-foot space features virtual reality, CD-ROM, and high-tech video games. Design incorporated larger-than-life kiosk fixtures, each featuring a different interactive computer game or adventure. Designed to easily accommodate changes and new technology, the fixtures are fabricated of MDF with a high-gloss automotive lacquer, with metal, foam, and plastic laminates. The retail store features fixtures of clear finished maple. A "Main Street" aisle of ceramic tile and inlaid geometric inserts leads visitors through the store to exhibits and eventually to the open plaza snack bar.

PHOTO: ALISE O'BRIEN, ST. LOUIS

Design Kiku Obata & Company, Inc.
Project Big Future Interactive Theme House
CLAYTON ROAD, ST. LOUIS, MISSOURI

Design Alexia N.C. Levite and Brian Levite, ▷
The Office of Alexia N.C. Levite

Neutral gray color values highlight the
merchandise in this retail gallery, and show off the
classic architecture.

PHOTO: BRUCE KATZ

Design John Lum Architecture ▽
Architect John Lum Architecture
Lighting John Lum Architecture
Project Urban Eyes Optometry Boutique #1
SAN FRANCISCO, CALIFORNIA

The challenge in trying on glasses is that the
lighting is not always conducive to looking one's
best. In this boutique, an economical solution is
fashioned from standard materials to create
backlit mirrors. First, eight-by-twelve inch squares
of mirror were sandblasted in a three-inch band
along the edges, and mounted on a pole. Step
lights mounted vertically in the columns behind
the mirrors provide flattering illumination. The
eyewear displays are lit from below, using
standard well lights mounted in the floor. Glare
shields direct illumination towards product and
away from customers' eyes.

Design Nora Fischer Designs ▶

Blue and white accented with black forms a scheme that is cool and modern. The geometric form of a corrugated silver display modulates the space and focuses attention on the merchandise.

PHOTO: MAX MACKENZIE

Design The Office of Alexia N.C. Levite ▼

Graded color hues add depth to a celestial blue-painted sky. The blue ceiling recedes from broken, creamy walls, giving the store an airy atmosphere.

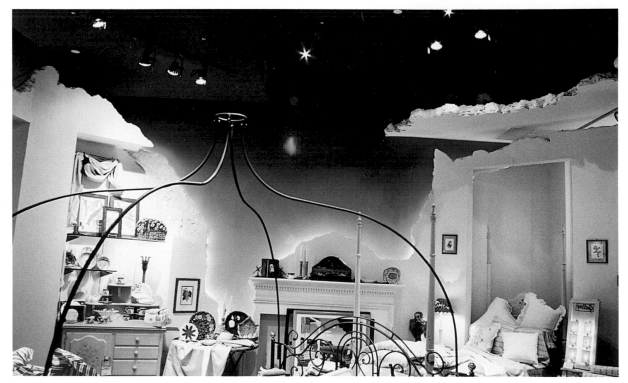

Directory

Design Forum *68-73*
7575 Paragon Road
Dayton, OH 45429
(937) 439-4400
fax: (937) 439-4340
e-mail: retail@ designforum.com

Fitzpatrick Design Group, Inc. *4-9, 24-29*
2109 Broadway #203
New York, NY 10023
(212) 580-5842
fax: (212) 580-5849

FRCH Design Worldwide *14-17, 30-37*
860 Broadway
New York, NY 10003
(212) 254-1229
fax: (212) 982-5543
e-mail: info@ frch.com

Haigh Architects *47*
125 Greenwich Avenue
Greenwich, CT 06830
(203) 869-5445
fax: (203) 869-5033
e-mail: tome4u@earthlink.net

Jencen Associates *46*
2850 Euclid Avenue
Cleveland, OH 44115
(216) 781-0131
fax: (216) 781-0134
e-mail: jerryr@prodigy.net

John Lum Architecture *13, 47, 78*
46 Alpine St., Suite 1
San Francisco, CA 94117
(415) 753-0339
fax: (415) 753-2233

Jon Greenberg & Associates *10-12,*
48-51, 52-53
29355 Northwestern Highway,
Suite 300
Southfield, MI 48034
(248) 355-0890
fax (248) 351-3062

Kiku Obata & Company *74-77*
5585 Pershing Ave., Suite 240
St. Louis, MO 63112
(314) 361-3110
fax: (314) 361-4716

Lee Stout, Inc. *62-63*
348 West 36 Street
New York, NY 10018
(212) 594-4563
fax: (212) 268-5579

Nora Fischer Designs Inc. *79*
2906 Cortland Place NW
Washington, DC 20008
(202) 265-8482
fax: (202) 265-8482
e-mail: Blanderman@aol.com

Ohashi Design *46*
5739 Presley Ave.
Oakland, A 94618
(510)652-8840
fax: (510) 652-8604
e-mail: ADS2000@aol.com

Pavlick Design Team *38-41, 42-45, 66-67*
1301 East Broward Bouleard
Fort Lauderdale, FL 33301
(954) 523-3300
fax: (954) 524-8370

Ronnette Riley Architect *58-61, 64-65*
350 fifth Ave #8001
New York, NY 10118-8099
(212) 594-4015
fax: (212) 594-2868
e-mail: rriley@pipeline.com

Schafer *18-23, 54-57*
635 Butterfiled IRd.
Oakbrook Terrace, IL 60181
(630) 932-8787
fax: (630) 932-8788
e-mail: SchaferUSA @ aol.com

The Office of Alexia N.C. Levite *78, 79*
3299 K Street, N.W., Suite 600
Washington, DC 20007
(202) 337-3987
fax: (202) 337-7583